USA TODAY BESTSELLING AUTHOR
PERSEPHONE AUTUMN

BENEATH
wildflowers

POETRY

&

PROSE

BENEATH WILDFLOWERS

A COLLECTION OF POETRY AND PROSE

PERSEPHONE AUTUMN

BETWEEN WORDS PUBLISHING LLC

Beneath Wildflowers

Copyright © 2023 by Persephone Autumn and Between Words Publishing LLC

www.persephoneautumn.com

All rights reserved.

No part of this book may be reproduced in any form or by any electronic or mechanical means, including photocopying, information storage and retrieval systems, without written permission from the author except for the use of brief quotations in a book review.

This book is a work of fiction. Names, characters, establishments, organizations, and incidents are either products of the author's imagination or are used fictitiously to give a sense of authenticity. Any resemblance to actual events, places, or persons, living or dead, is entirely coincidental.

If you're reading this book and did not purchase it, or it was not purchased for your use only, or it was purchased on a site I do not advertise I sell on, then it was pirated illegally. Please purchase a copy of your own on a platform where the author advertises she distributes and respect the hard work of this author.

ISBN: 978-1-951477-69-1 (Ebook)

ISBN: 978-1-951477-70-7 (Paperback)

Editor: Ellie McLove | My Brother's Editor

Cover Design: Abigail Davies | Pink Elephant Designs

BOOKS BY PERSEPHONE AUTUMN

Lake Lavender Series

Depths Awakened

One Night Forsaken

Every Thought Taken

Devotion Series

Distorted Devotion

Undying Devotion

Beloved Devotion

Darkest Devotion

Sweetest Devotion

Bay Area Duet Series

Click Duet

Through the Lens

Time Exposure

Inked Duet

Fine Line

Love Buzz

Insomniac Duet

Restless Night

A Love So Bright

Artist Duet

Blank Canvas

Abstract Passion

Novellas

Reese

Penny

Stone Bay Series

Broken Sky—Prequel

Shattered Sun

Standalone Romance Novels

Sweet Tooth

Transcendental

Poetry Collections

Ink Veins

Broken Metronome

Slipping From Existence

Poisonous Heart

Beneath Wildflowers

PUBLISHED UNDER P. AUTUMN

Standalone Non-Romance Novels

By Dawn

For my little mister, my main squeeze, the only guy to hold all of my heart in his little paws. My Shadow.
I miss you like hell, little man.

FIRST NIGHT

You were a surprise
on a warm summer night.
The sweetest, most precious surprise.

In cupped hands,
I held you
close to my heart
Stroked
your soft fur
Melted
at your squeaky cry

To think someone didn't
want you
To think someone literally
tossed you away
and left you
abandoned in a dumpster

They didn't know

your sweet and tender soul
They didn't know
you had the biggest heart

On that first night
even when life was
busy
difficult
straining at times,
you brought light into my life.
You gifted me with love
I didn't realize I was missing.
You gave me a reason
to smile.

MEET SHADOW

Not a single cat of my past compared to you, my sweet Shadow. When you were gifted your name, it wasn't because you followed me or anyone else from room to room. In those early days, you had darker fur. More black than brown. You simply mirrored a shadow. Back then, no one knew your name would suit you so properly. That you would become *my* shadow. The little man that never left my side. The guy weaving between my legs or cozy in my arms. And the only guy to truly steal my heart.

PILLOW CUDDLES

You gave new meaning to
cuddle buddy.

With your loud, happy purring
you curled up each night
next to my head.
Like I was your
protector
and you were
mine.

Such tiny paws
you kneaded me with
soft pads and
sharp claws

I endured those
makeshift acupuncture sessions
stroking your fur

whispering sweet, loving words
as you tangled my hair

Little did I know,
these cuddles would be
what I miss most.

FETCH AND PLAY

All my life
I'd never met a cat
like you

You were more than
a cat
You were this
light
peace
burst of joy
warmth I'd been missing

And you loved to play
But your version of play
was unlike any other cat

You were picky
Only liked a certain brand of toy
Only liked certain sizes of toys
You did care for

feathers
bells
ordinary things

No, my boy loved small toys
noiseless toys
toys he could bite and hold in his mouth
toys I could easily toss and he could fetch
toys that looked like a bone in his mouth
as if he were part dog

Shadow…
the only cat I've known to fetch and play
over and over and over

Oh, how I miss our playtime
Oh, how I miss your unique soul

CALLING FOR MOM

I didn't believe it until I heard it with my own ears. My Shadow called out for his mom—me. In the beginning, I was told it happened when I left home. He'd watch me leave, go sit by the door, and cry out *Mom*, over and over. He did this for minutes, possibly hours. Then one day, I heard his sweet cry. *Mom*. I was doing something out of view, and my guy was looking for me. *Mom*. He said the three-letter word in his raspy meow, and my heart melted.

He was my Shadow, and I'd always be Mom.

THROUGH TOUGH TIMES

Life got a little rocky
it was time for change
dramatic change
change that twists your stomach in knots
change that makes you dizzy
change that has the world wobbly

But through those tough times
you were one of my few constants
you loved me unconditionally
you gifted me with snuggles and smiles

And anytime I go through a rough patch
I think of you
and how you loved me

MAIN SQUEEZE

Of all the souls in my life
it was easy gifting you this title

Main Squeeze

You had always been
more than a cat
my greatest companion
the main man in my heart
mine

You loved me like no other
unconditionally
fiercely
effortlessly

And even on the days
when you misbehaved
I loved you the same

My Main Squeeze

SNUGGLE BUDDY

I've always been weird about physical affection. Not because I don't enjoy it. Not because something traumatic steered me away from it. I've just always felt I wasn't *good* at affection. Like I don't know how to express myself —verbally or physically.

But you changed all of that. You were persistent.

Night after night, year after year, you refused to be anything except my snuggle buddy. The first half of your life, you curled up on my pillow, owned half the space, and nestled in my hair. Your sweet purrs echoed in my ear until you fell asleep. And as you grew older, you snuggled against my side with your head next to mine on the pillow. We slept under the covers, my arm hooked around the length of you.

I haven't snuggled with many in my life. And I love that I snuggled you the most. It just makes those memories more precious.

PARROT

In my desk chair
On the couch
In any seat, really
you always found a way to be close

One of my favorites
was when you perched on my shoulders
like a bird
like a parrot

You'd sit there for
minutes
hours
until I got up

All you wanted was
to be close
to let me know you were near
to have some form of physical contact

And while I worked or read or watched television
I leaned into your proximity
snuggled into your warm fur
gave you dozens of kisses
scratched behind your ears

Those little parrot moments were
sweet and subtle
some of my favorite moments

I miss those parrot moments.

CHASING LEAVES

I remember the first time
the leaves excited you.

In early spring,
when the breeze picked up
more often than not,
you sat on the small table under the window,
looking for squirrels and birds.
Then the wind gusted
and kicked up the oak leaves.

I'd never heard you meow like you did with the leaves.
A stuttered and almost silent meow.
Like you worried about scaring them away.

For as long as the wind stirred up the leaves,
for as long as they fluttered in the air,
you sat on your perch
you swatted the window
you mewled that raspy cry of excitement.

And I sat on the couch with rapt attention,
not wanting to miss a single second of your joy.

COWORKER

To say you always wanted
to be at my side
to be wherever I was
is an understatement

When life gifted me the opportunity
to be home more
you took full advantage of the time.

As I started a new career,
I also started writing more.
Days at the desk,
on the couch,
you were there…
my sweet coworker.
Curling up in my lap.
Snuggling beside my stretched-out legs.
In my space
always near
my constant

And when I tried to snap "work photos"
you tolerated my antics
you leaned in close
you posed for the camera

Although you made work more challenging
as I finagled around you,
I miss those moments
I wish for more of those moments
working isn't the same without you.

You were my favorite coworker,
always loving me when it was a tough day.

SOUL MATE

What is a soul mate? By definition, a soul mate is a person ideally suited to another as a close friend or romantic partner. But I have a different definition of soul mate. One that isn't limited to human souls.

Because you were definitely one of my soul mates.

In my eyes, a soul mate is a soul you are tethered to, in this life, previous lives, and all lives that follow. Soul mates aren't limited by physical form. Human, cat, dog, any soul-bearing creature.
I've never known a soul as sweet and loving and giving as yours. We may not have spoken the same language, but we didn't need to. I felt your love every time you called out for me. Every time you chose me over everyone else. Every time you snuggled my side or gave me your version of kisses.

You loved me in a way only a soul mate could—fully and unconditionally.

And I loved you just the same.

DID YOU SAY DINNER?

I've always been
the strait-laced pet parent.
The one that didn't give
table scraps
excessive snacks
too many treats

But you got your share of them all
Just not from me

Not long after you gained a second mom
you learned to effectively beg
for what I would never give
and get little nibbles from another mom's plate

It became a nightly ritual
to beg for food that was not yours.
Though I never
caved
handed over scraps

it was adorable and funny to watch.
And now that you're no longer here
to cry for a pizza crust
to swat for cheese
to dance for veggies
I miss those chaotic dinners.

I miss you ignoring your own food
for the chance at mere crumbs of ours.
I miss the constant need
to guard my plate
because you danced from left to right behind me.
I miss the way you made me laugh
for something so simple
because it was something other than your boring food.

The funniest thing of all is
you never begged for any other meal.
For whatever reason,
dinner was the magic meal.

And dinner isn't the same without you.

MISS YOUR KISSES

Not a year of my life has existed without a cat. Many were sweet and affectionate. But none were like you and the way you showed love.

I miss your kisses. How you pressed your nose to mine and rubbed the tip of my nose with yours. How you'd rub from your nose to your cheek over my nose. How you eventually pressed your little mouth to mine.

The way you loved me, it was a running joke that you were my boyfriend. Maybe my husband.

You gifted only me with your kisses. Not because you didn't love anyone else. But because you loved me the most, and those kisses—your kisses—were one of a kind. Just like you.

I miss your kisses, almost as much as I miss you.

MR. PICKY

Who knew
cats could be so picky

Looking back on it,
I confess my guy was a toy snob.
Over the years,
I bought you countless toys
I watched you ignore the jingling bells
I laughed at your fussy nature

Most cats would play with any toy,
but not you.
You looked at me like I was
out of my mind
ridiculous
laughable
…until I discovered your favorite brand.

Bright and vibrant,
colorful and small,

it was love at first sight.

I tossed the toy
in the hopes you'd simply
play with it
swat it
kick it
bite it

Then you picked it up
You brought it to me
You meowed, asking me to throw it again.
You—my cat—played fetch,
and it was the cutest damn thing.

We named each and every one of those toys.
You loved them,
played with them without provocation,
tossed them in the air and swatted them on the way down,
pounced them then did that back foot kick thing I'll never forget.

You loved those toys,
especially *hot dog,*
who now sits next to where you rest
so you can still play with him wherever you are.

CURTAIN CALL

So many memories of you
are profound in my mind
because you had an unforgettable personality

But to this day,
I still miss you between the curtains.

Like your name suggested,
you were my shadow,
always following me room to room.
But something about shower time…
it isn't the same without you.

I miss the way you jumped between the curtains
when I cranked on the water
I miss how you sat there and waited,
not wanting to miss a single moment with me
I miss how you occasionally
peeked around the liner,
needing to see me

needing to know I was still there

And as you got older,
I miss how you jumped in the tub
after the water turned off
to lick water droplets off the tub

Sometimes, I still look for you
between the curtains
even though I know you're not there

Sometimes, I stay in the shower longer
with my eyes closed
wishing you were there

NEVER LOVED ANYONE LIKE YOU

It's quite possible I'll never love anyone the way I loved you.

Is that weird? Is that wrong?

Regardless, I don't care.

For so many difficult years in my life, you were there. You loved me without reservation. You wanted nothing but love in return. And you were my constant and my loyal companion. You lifted me up when I was low. Refused to let me be sad by giving me constant kisses.

Aside from Dad, you were the only guy in my life to never let me down.

How could I ever love anyone the way I loved you? It's not possible.

OLD MAN

Watching a spry kitten
become a mature cat
then an old man
is peculiar

Even as I saw the changes…
more white fur on his face
weight loss without diet restriction
the way you walked a little different
those darn wrist snaps
…I didn't want to believe you were aging.

Though you still loved me fiercely
as you aged
you spent less time with me

And it saddened my heart
seeing those changes
because they meant something I didn't
and still don't

want to think.

Our time was limited.

Nevertheless, I loved you
I scooped you up like a scoop of ice cream
I held you often and close
I kissed you and told you how much I love you

With limited time,
all those moments
all the snuggles and kisses and words
hold more value

Because you never know when you won't have them anymore.

Growing old is inevitable.
So I used every second to make
final memories of you.
Memories I will never forget.

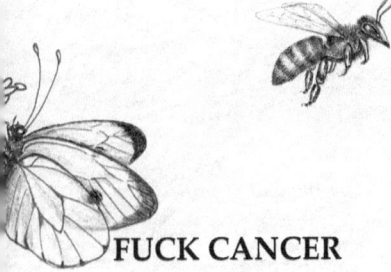

FUCK CANCER

You weren't well, and I didn't know why.

At dinner, you'd eat as if starved, then later throw it up. Whenever food appeared, whether yours or ours, you cried more than usual. Begging. Pleading for something to eat. You'd lost so much weight and were constantly ravenous.

We took you to the vet. Your first visit in far too long. Oftentimes, I wonder if I'd taken you sooner, maybe we would've known sooner. Maybe we could've changed things or started things earlier. Before it was too late.

A week after that visit, things were better. We'd made minor changes and life was looking up.

You were happier, perkier, acting years younger.

But that didn't last long. The same symptoms crept back up. You were more isolated, reserved, solemn. And I knew the answer as to why you were hurting wouldn't be good.

And after another trip to the vet, we learned you had cancer. It invaded your small body. Ate away at your happiness and health. Stole the little glimpses of light you had left in your sixteen year old body.

We could've said yes to chemo. Could've done countless treatments to keep you for a few extra months.

But I said no.

I didn't want the end of your life to be more painful. I didn't want you to go through all that agony to live three to six months more, doing nothing but lying around.

I didn't want to lose you, but I hated that you were in pain more.

Fuck cancer.

Fuck the pain it causes.

Fuck the lives it takes too soon.

GOODBYE

I haven't said goodbye
to many in my life.
But saying goodbye to you,
was the hardest goodbye yet.

August twenty-seventh, two-thousand-twenty-one.
I will never forget that day.

You knew something was wrong,
you knew something was different
when we got in the car.
You wanted out of that carrier.
You refused treats.
You didn't cry as you normally did in the car.

I tried not to cry during that drive.
I tried to comfort you,
to not let you feel my heart breaking
as we got closer to goodbye.

I still remember the soft blanket
they had draped over the cat bed
and the way you cried when we took you out of the carrier.

You knew it was goodbye,
and neither of us wanted to say it.

I'm still so sorry
I left the room early.
Much as I wanted to stay,
much as I wanted to be there
until the very end,
I couldn't stay.

Of all the photographic memories
I wanted to keep of you,
I didn't want the very end to be
all I saw when I remembered your sweet face.

So I sat in the car,
crying
shaking
rocking
whispering how much I loved you
wishing I could've been stronger and stayed
beating my chest, over my heart, and saying
one last goodbye

I hate that I had to say goodbye,
but I'm glad you're no longer in pain.

RAINBOW BRIDGE

I like to think of
The Rainbow Bridge
as the path to
happiness
freedom
a soft place to play
until we meet again

I picture you there,
frolicking in grass
chasing leaves and squirrels and birds
playing fetch with *hot dog*
seeing long lost friends again
like Kiki and Anakin and Sami

I picture you happy
while you wait for me
to meet you in the next life

Fuck, how I miss you.

But I know we will meet again.
We will love again.
And I look forward to loving you just as intensely
in the next life.

STILL HERE

The tears come less often,
two years later,
but I know you are
still here
still with me
still sleeping by my side each night

I only cry on the
hard days
when I wish you were here
to kiss and snuggle me better

Most days,
I recall the happy memories
and smile.

Some would think me strange
for petting your urn
for talking to you while I fold the laundry
for kissing your picture

two years later.

Though I try to focus on only the good,
I can't help but cry
from time to time,
wishing you were still here.

On the toughest days,
I pull up videos,
forever grateful I have them,
and watch you play or just be that
lovable guy
I got sixteen incredible years with.

My main squeeze.
My soul mate.
My heart.
My Shadow.

I will love you forever,
and I can't wait to
hold
snuggle
kiss
and love you again.

Love you forever,
Mom

MORE BY PERSEPHONE

Ink Veins

Persephone Autumn's debut poetry collection, Ink Veins, explores topics of depression, love, and self-discovery with a raw, unfiltered voice.

Broken Metronome

When the music of the heart dies…

Broken Metronome is an angsty poetry collection full of heartache and the possibility of what may have been.

Slipping From Existence

Would it be so bad to slip from existence? Would it be so bad to give in to the darkness?

Slipping From Existence is a dark poetry collection centered around depression and coping while maintaining a brave face.

Poisonous Heart

Drip fed, little by little, I was young when I got my first taste of poison.

Small doses in heart-shaped packages labeled as love.

I don't remember the very first taste. But that's how poison works.

Depths Awakened

A small town romance which captivates you from the start. Mags and Geoff are two broken souls who have sworn off love. Vowed to never lose anyone else. But their undeniable attraction brings them together and refuses to let go.

Every Thought Taken

As young children, an unshakable friendship brought them together. As teens, they discovered an undeniable love. Then life pulled them in different directions–into darkness and light–and slowly ripped them apart. Years later, he returns home in the hopes of a second chance with his first love and to conquer the demons of his past.

Distorted Devotion

Free-spirited Sarah lives life to the fullest. When a new love interest enters her life, she starts receiving strange gifts and letters. She doesn't want to relinquish her freedom or new love, but fears the consequences.

Transcendental

A musician in search of his muse and a woman grieving the loss of her husband. Two weeks at an exclusive retreat and their connection rivals all others. Until she leaves early without notice. But he refuses to give up until he finds her again.

The Click Duet

High school sweethearts torn apart. When fate gives them a second chance, one doesn't trust they won't be hurt again. Through the Lens (Click Duet #1) and Time Exposure (Click Duet #2) is an angsty, second chance, friends to lovers romance with all the feels.

The Inked Duet

A man with a broken heart and a woman scared to put herself out there. Love is never easy. Sometimes love rips you apart. Fine

Line (Inked Duet #1) and Love Buzz (Inked Duet #2) is a second chance at love, single parent romance with a pinch of angst and dash of suspense.

The Insomniac Duet

He was her high school bully. She was the outcast that secretly crushed on him. More than ten years later, he's her boss, completely oblivious to their shared past, and wants no one but her. More importantly, he doesn't understand her animosity toward him.

The Artist Duet

A tortured hero with the biggest heart and a charismatic heroine with the patience of a saint. Previous heartache has him fighting his desire to be more than friends with her. But she is everywhere, and he can't help but give in. The Artist Duet is an angsty, friends to lovers slow burn.

Broken Sky

Their eyes meet across the bar, but she looks away first. Does her best to give him zero attention. But when he crowds her on the dancefloor, she can't deny the instant chemistry. After one night together, he marks her as his. Unfortunately, another woman thinks he belongs to her.

THANK YOU

Thank you so much for reading **Beneath Wildflowers**. If you wouldn't mind taking a moment to leave a review on the retailer site where you made your purchase, Goodreads and/or BookBub, it would mean the world to me.

Reviews help other readers find and enjoy the book as well.

Much love,
    Persephone

CONNECT WITH PERSEPHONE

Connect with Persephone
www.persephoneautumn.com

Subscribe to Persephone's newsletter
www.persephoneautumn.com/newsletter

Join Persephone's reader's group
Persephone's Playground

Follow Persephone online

- instagram.com/persephoneautumn
- facebook.com/persephoneautumnwrites
- tiktok.com/@persephoneautumn
- bookbub.com/authors/persephone-autumn
- goodreads.com/persephoneautumn
- amazon.com/author/persephoneautumn
- pinterest.com/persephoneautumn

ACKNOWLEDGMENTS

To my family... Thank you for your endless support and cheering me on through this author journey! This poetry collection was by far the most difficult to write. I cried so damn hard my eyes were puffy and vision blurry an entire 24 hours.

Ellie at My Brother's Editor! Thank you for all you do. My books wouldn't be what they are without your expertise.

Abi of Pink Elephant Designs! Thank you for another gorgeous cover. Though this was a premade, it was exactly what I needed for this project—one held the closest to my heart.

Author peeps... I love you! This business is rough and exhausting, but I love how we lean on and support each other. To belong to a community where every person wants everyone to thrive and succeed... I love it and you!

Readers are the best humans! Thank you to each and every one of you for reading my words. For choosing one of my books, thank you times a million. If I could hug you all, my tentacle arms would squeeze you tight.

ABOUT THE AUTHOR

USA Today Bestselling Author Persephone Autumn lives in Florida with her wife and psycho cat. A proud mom with a cuckoo grandpup. An ethnic food enthusiast who has fun discovering ways to vegan-ize her favorite non-vegan foods. Most days, you'll find her with a tea latte or fruity concoction in her hand. If given the opportunity, she would intentionally get lost in nature.

For years, Persephone did some form of writing; mostly journaling or poetry. After pairing her poetry with images and posting them online, she began the journey of writing her first novel.

She mainly writes romance and poetry, but on occasion dips her toes in other works. Look for her non-romance publications under P. Autumn.

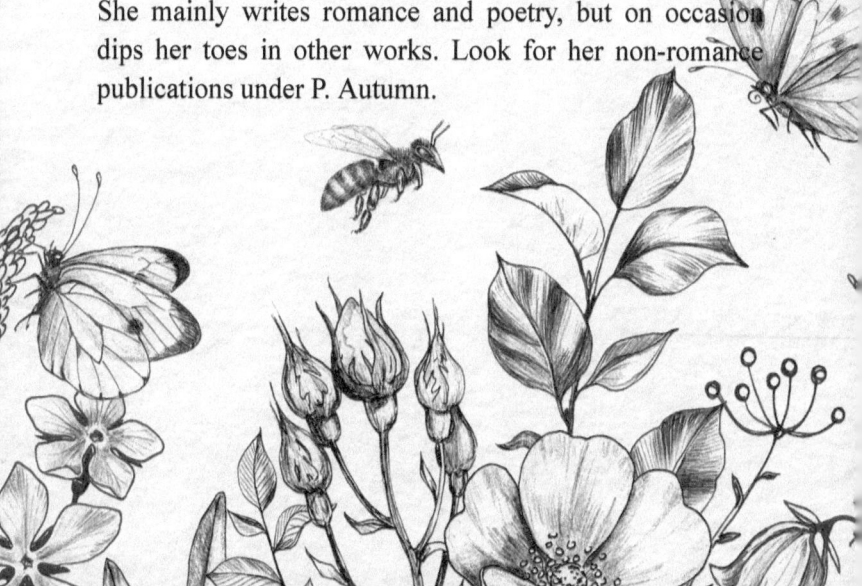

www.ingramcontent.com/pod-product-compliance
Lightning Source LLC
Chambersburg PA
CBHW030139100526
44592CB00011B/968